Goldendoodle

Golden Retriever

Bulldog

American eskimo dog

Boston Terrier

Labrador retriever

Siberian Husky

Weimaraner

Havanese

Great Dane

Beagle

Dachsund

German Shepherd

Poodle

Australian Shepherd

Maltese

Rottweiler

Chihuahua

Doberman

Pug

Boxer

Bernese Mountain Dog

Newfoundland

Shiba Inu

Collie

Dalmatian

Schnauzer

St. Bernard

Vizsla

Jack Russel Terrier

Komondor

Afghan Hound

Shih Tzu

Chow Chow

Bedlington Terrier

Tibetan Spaniel

Keeshond

Korean Jindo Dog

Bichon Frise